BASEBALL and BELONGING

Written by **Ryan Lavarnway**

World Series Champion & Olympian

Illustrated by **Chris Brown**

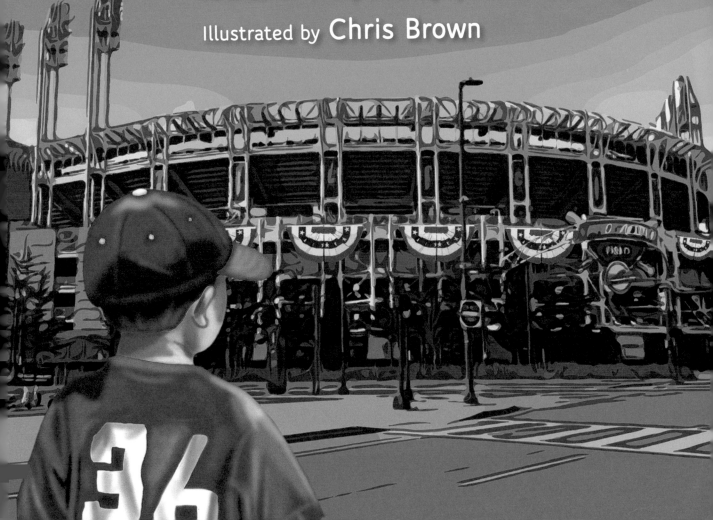

Baseball and Belonging
Published by Turn Left LLC
Englewood, CO

ISBN: 979-8-218-22743-2
JUVENILE NONFICTION / Sports & Recreation / Baseball & Softball

Cover and interior design by Victoria Wolf, wolfdesignandmarketing.com, copyright owned by Ryan Lavarnway.
Cover art and Illustrations by Chris Brown. Website: chrisbrownsportsart.net.

To my daughter, Blake.
May you always know where you belong.

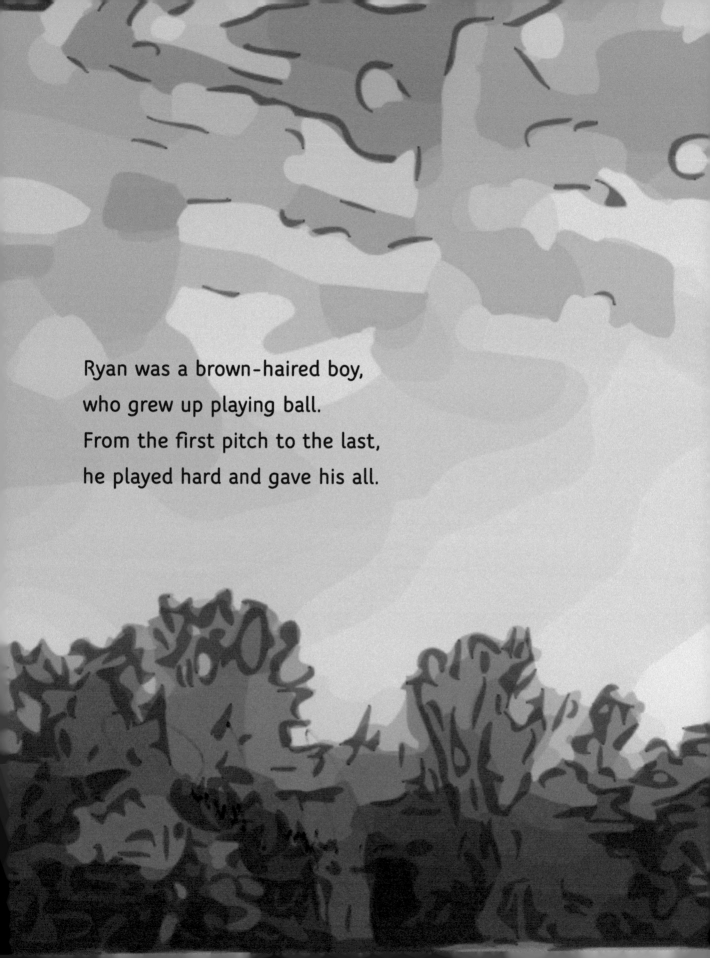

Ryan was a brown-haired boy,
who grew up playing ball.
From the first pitch to the last,
he played hard and gave his all.

Leather glove, spikes on his feet,
big number on his back.
Long wooden bat in his hands,
he swung hard and heard it whack!

The game taught him how to hit,
to catch and throw and run.

It taught him how to win and lose,
to share and always have fun.

Ryan loved his teammates,
and they hung out off the field.
They talked about their lives and faith
during celebrations and meals.

Often times his teammates would invite him excitedly to join their church or temple and build community.

Ryan has a Jewish mom
and a Catholic dad.
He felt like he had to pick one;
he was confused and sad.

His parents let him choose his path.
They said, "You can be either."
But thinking he was half and half
made him feel like he was neither.

The place he knew he did belong
was on a baseball field.
Religion felt uncertain;
but to him baseball felt real.

Ryan kept avoiding faith
and stuck to what he loved.
He excelled on the field,
both with his bat and glove.

Time passed, and he felt something
was missing from his heart.
He wanted faith and meaning;
he wondered where to start.

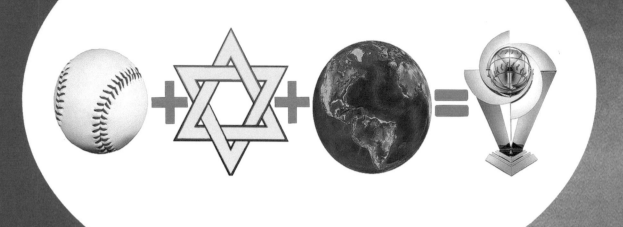

One day he was asked to join
a Jewish baseball team
in a worldwide tournament.
It was the answer to his dreams.

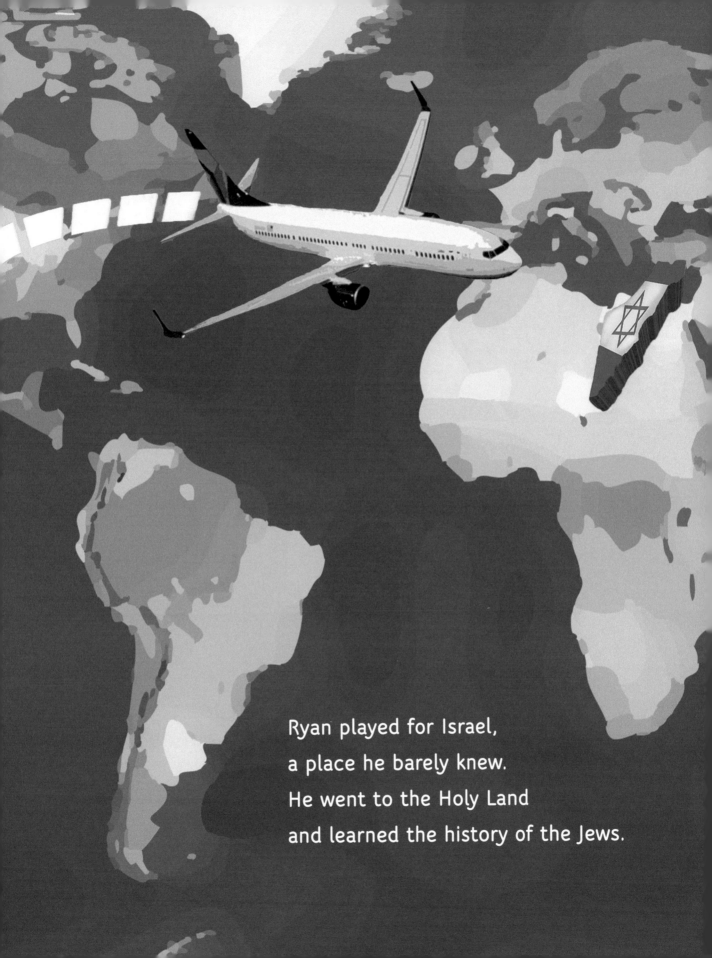

Ryan played for Israel,
a place he barely knew.
He went to the Holy Land
and learned the history of the Jews.

He saw Independence Hall,
rode bikes in Tel Aviv.

He went to the Western Wall,
and floated in the Dead Sea.

He rode on a camel's back,
took a Masada hike,

paid tribute at Yad Vashem,
saw Jerusalem at night.

He met Israeli kids
who came from near and far.
They looked up to the players
like they were superstars.

More than anything he felt
a growing sense of pride.
People said, "You're one of us.
Welcome to the tribe!"

The tournament started;
the other teams were strong.
No one thought Israel could win,
but they were proven wrong.

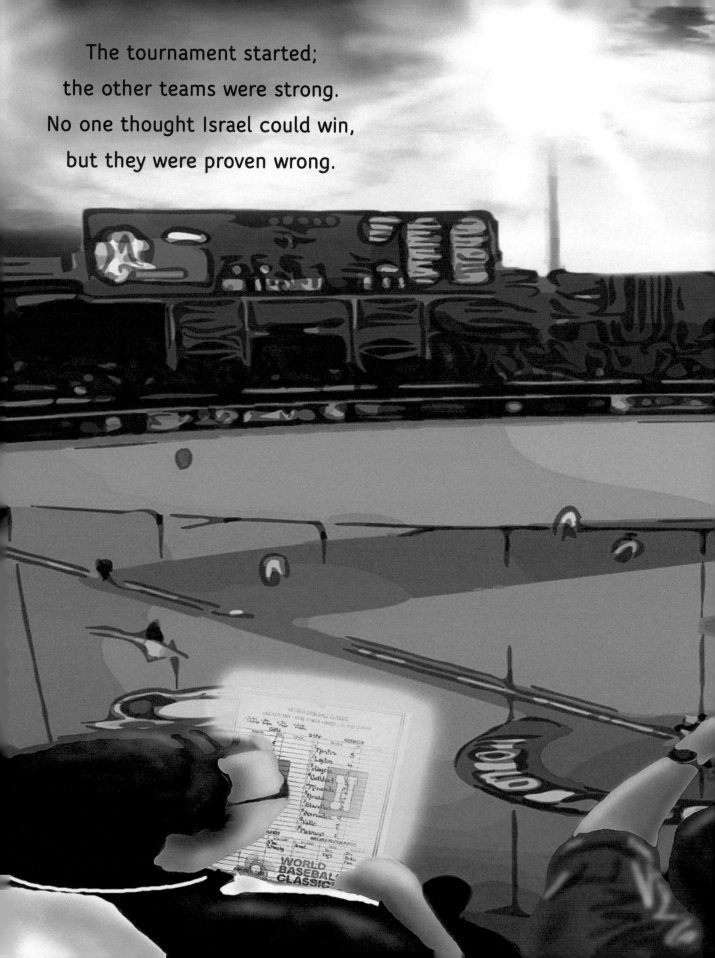

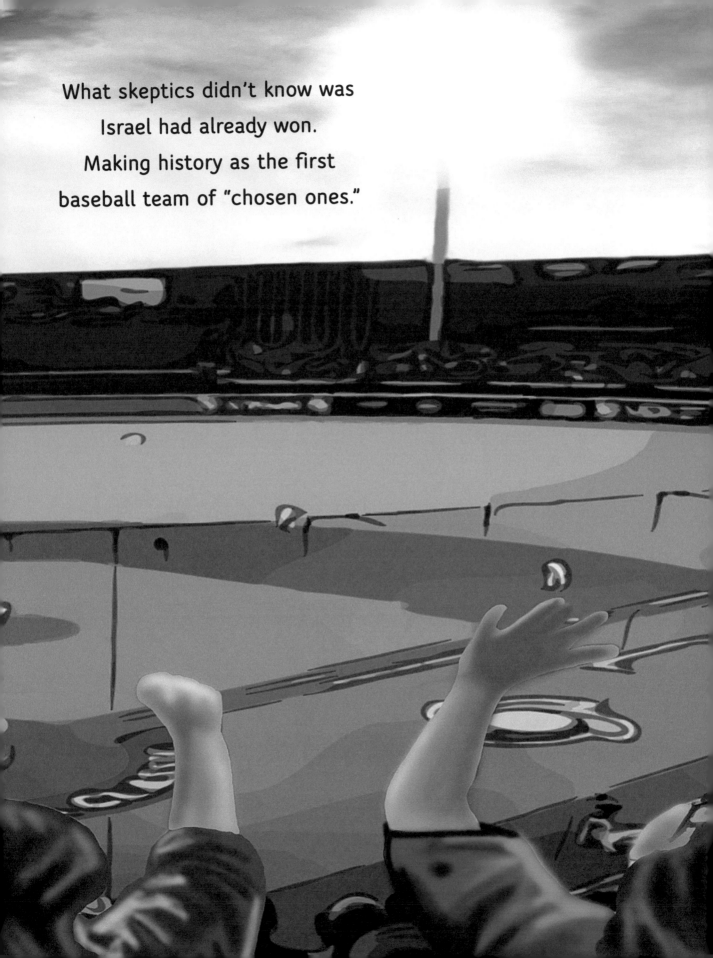

What skeptics didn't know was
Israel had already won.
Making history as the first
baseball team of "chosen ones."

Fans cheered when the players
replaced their hats with kippot.
Hatikvah was their anthem;
it filled their hearts with hope.

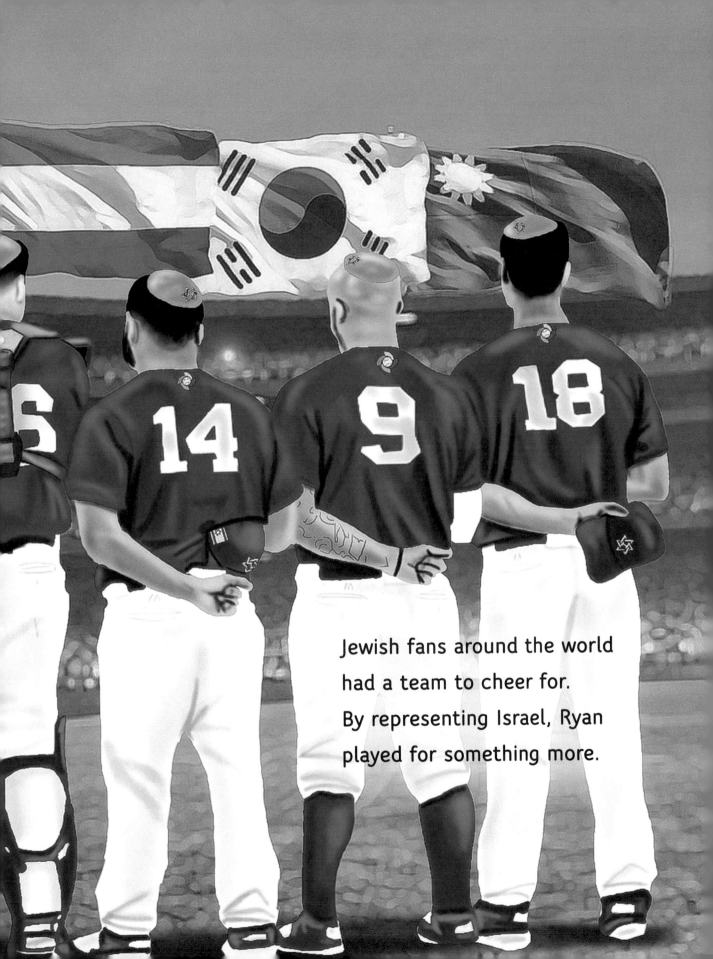

Jewish fans around the world
had a team to cheer for.
By representing Israel, Ryan
played for something more.

Team Israel gave its all,
and Ryan did the same.
The team shocked the entire world
and won its first four games.

Team Israel had a following
of fans from different faiths.
People across the globe applauded
when Team Israel took sixth place.

Instead of feeling half and half,
Ryan finally felt whole.
"I am Jewish; I am proud!"
He could feel it in his soul.

Playing with Team Israel,
was just the very start.
Ryan found where he belonged,
on the field and in his heart.

For More Understanding

History of Israel

On May 14, 1948, Israel declared independence and became a self-governing country in the modern world. Israel's citizenship requirements are defined by the Law of Return. The law grants Jews, individuals with a Jewish heritage, and their immediate family members the right to make "Aliyah," (immigrate to Israel) and obtain Israeli citizenship. It symbolizes Israel's commitment to provide a safe haven for Jews worldwide, regardless of their current nationality. Israel will also extend citizenship to non-Jews in certain circumstances.

History of WBC

The World Baseball Classic (WBC) was first held in 2006 and has since taken place every four years. It is similar to the World Cup in other sports.

In order to give countries that are not known for baseball a chance to compete, the WBC allows players to represent a country as long as they qualify to obtain citizenship. Participants are not required to have active citizenship and a valid passport from the country they represent.

History of Team Israel

In 2012, Peter Kurz, the president of the Israel Association of Baseball, used the World Baseball Classic's heritage-based entry requirements to recruit Jewish-American professional baseball players to represent Israel in the tournament.

In September of 2016, Israel earned the right to enter the WBC. At that time, Israel had just one baseball field in the entire country and was ranked sixty-fourth in the world. The team surprised critics and fans alike with a Cinderella run to finish the tournament in sixth place after eliminating teams fielded by South Korea (ranked third), Cuba (ranked fourth), Chinese Taipei (ranked sixth), and the Netherlands (ranked eleventh).

Following their success in the WBC, Israel went on to qualify for the 2021 Olympics and finished in fifth place.

The prize money the team won funded two more baseball fields in Israel. As of the publication of this book, a third field is being built. Participation in baseball has more than doubled within Israel, and Team Israel has become a mainstay in international competitions.

Independence Hall

Independence Hall, located in Tel Aviv, Israel, is the site where David Ben-Gurion, the first Prime Minister of Israel, read aloud the Declaration of Independence in 1948.

Independence Hall is a symbol of hope and resilience. It represents the miraculous emergence of the modern state against significant odds.

Masada Hike

Masada is an ancient fortress that was constructed by King Herod the Great in the first century BCE. In 73–74 CE, the invading Roman army laid siege to Masada, and ultimately overtook it. Although the Romans overtook the fortress, the people stood strong and fought bravely to the end.

The story of Masada has become a symbol of Jewish resilience and defiance against oppression. It represents the unwavering commitment to freedom and the refusal to submit to tyranny, even in the face of overwhelming odds.

Dead Sea

At 1,412 feet below sea level, the Dead Sea is Earth's lowest point on land.

It is one of the saltiest bodies of water on Earth. It gets its name from its high salt concentration, which makes it inhospitable for most marine life. This unique feature allows swimmers to effortlessly float on its surface.

Yad Vashem

Yad Vashem is Israel's National Holocaust Museum. It was established in 1953.

The museum provides a somber reflection on the importance of actively combating anti-Semitism along with advocating for human rights and social justice.

Western Wall

The Western Wall is an outer remnant of the ancient Jewish temple complex that stood on the Temple Mount over 2,000 years ago.

For Jews, the Western Wall is one of the holiest sites in the world. It is considered a place of profound spiritual connection and reflection on what was, is, and could be.

Acknowledgments

To my wife, Jamie — thank you for reading, reading again, and editing all along the way.

Chris Brown — your talent turned ideas into reality, and your art helps convey the story in a way that words alone never could.

Rabbi Joe Black — thank you for encouraging me to put my story into writing.

Peter Kurz — without you there is no story to tell. Thank you for bringing me onto Team Israel and giving me an experience that changed my life.

Ira Gewanter — thank you for helping me edit, improve and work through three different iterations of this book. Your support through everything means so much.

And finally, thank you to Amanda Miller, Shelly Wilhelm, and Victoria Wolf — *Baseball and Belonging* wouldn't be the same without your thoughtful improvements.

About the Illustrator

Chris Brown is a former Minor League Baseball player turned renowned professional artist. Since 2009, Chris has been the artist for the Louisiana Sports Hall of Fame in Natchitoches and has created portraits for each HOF inductee. He has also created designs for the Sugar Bowl and College Sports Weekly. You can visit Chris and learn about his children's book called Life Lessons from the Diamond at chrisbrownsportsart.net.

About the Author

Ryan Lavarnway played Major League Baseball for ten seasons over a fifteen-year career and was a member of the 2013 World Series-winning Boston Red Sox. In 2017 and 2023, Ryan represented Israel in the World Baseball Classic. In 2020, he played for Israel in the Olympic Games. In addition to his outstanding baseball career, Ryan is a father, husband, and proud member of the Jewish community. You can visit him at www.RyanLavarnway.com.

Ryan Lavarnway's story is both powerful and entertaining.

There's no better way to hear it than from Ryan himself.

Through heartfelt storytelling, Ryan's unique speaking style will leave your audience inspired to embrace their own journey toward faith and self-discovery by empowering them with the tools and mindset for exploring all facets of their lives.

Ryan has spoken to dozens of audiences around the country at faith-based, corporate, and team events.

Sometimes serious—sometimes funny—always compelling. Ryan's message encourages audiences to follow their passions and question their limitations.

To book Ryan for your event, please contact: lavarnway@unrivaledgroup.com
Or visit: www.RyanLavarnway.com

Made in the USA
Columbia, SC
01 March 2024